How to Be an
ANCIENT GREEK
WARRIOR

by Catherine M. Andronik

PEBBLE
a capstone imprint

Pebble is published by Capstone,
1710 Roe Crest Drive, North Mankato, Minnesota 56003
capstonepub.com

Copyright © 2026 by Capstone. All rights reserved. No part of this publication may be reproduced in whole or in part, or stored in a retrieval system, or transmitted in any form or by any means, electronic, mechanical, photocopying, recording, or otherwise, without written permission of the publisher.

Library of Congress Cataloging-in-Publication Data is available on the Library of Congress website.

ISBN: 9798875226847 (hardcover)
ISBN: 9798875234576 (paperback)
ISBN: 9798875234583 (ebook PDF)

Summary: Do you have what it takes to be an ancient Greek warrior?

Editorial Credits
Editor: Alison Deering; Designer: Bobbie Nuytten; Media Researcher: Svetlana Zhurkin; Production Specialist: Whitney Schaefer

Image Credits
Alamy: Archive Collection, 24, Les Archives Digitales, 25, North Wind Picture Archives, 9; Bridgeman images: © Look and Learn, 27, 28, Photo © Leonard de Selva, 12, Photo © North Wind Pictures, 29; Getty Images: mikroman6, 5, 6, 15, 22, NSA Digital Archive, 10; Shutterstock: 3DMI, 17, adolf martinez soler (stone wall), cover and throughout, Liliya Butenko, 18, Massimo Todaro, 7, 11, 14, 19, 21, Mikhail Hoika, 16, 23, See U in History, 13, Tomas Marek, cover (top), Vaclav Stastny, cover (bottom), Yip Po Yu (texture), cover and throughout

Any additional websites and resources referenced in this book are not maintained, authorized, or sponsored by Capstone. All product and company names are trademarks™ or registered® trademarks of their respective holders.

Table of Contents

Introduction
Welcome to Ancient Greece 4

Chapter 1
Hoping to Be a Hoplite? 6

Chapter 2
Training and Weapons 12

Chapter 3
Phalanx Power 20

Chapter 4
Ready for Battle? 26

Greek Warrior Test 30

Glossary 31

Index 32

About the Author 32

Words in **bold** are in the glossary.

Introduction

Welcome to Ancient Greece

Let's journey back in time to 800 BCE. In the western part of the Mediterranean, the Greek empire was a major power. But Greece was not a unified country. It was made up of **city-states**. Each city-state had its own ruler, laws, and customs. And each had its own army.

Sometimes, the Greek city-states went to war with one another. Other times, they united against a common enemy. But no matter the battle, they needed plenty of warriors.

Greek warriors were strong, brave, and willing to do anything to defend their home. Do YOU have what it takes to be an ancient Greek warrior?

Chapter 1

Hoping to Be a Hoplite?

The city-states of Greece are close together, but they do not always get along. Sometimes the differences are political. The city-state of Athens is a **democracy**. Sparta, another powerful city-state, is ruled by kings.

Athens

Sometimes city-states claim rights to the same resource, like fresh water. Sometimes they do not like the way others try to control their neighbors.

There are political **alliances** among the city-states. These often fall apart. When that happens, warriors from one city-state fight against those from another.

In most of the city-states, soldier is not a profession. Free adult men are expected to serve two years in their local **militia** without pay. Most complete their service in their youth. These foot soldiers are called **hoplites**, which comes from the Greek word for "shield" or "weapon."

To become a hoplite, you must be able to answer YES to the following questions:

1. Are you male?
2. Are you a free citizen?
3. Are you between the ages of 13 and 60?
4. Can you buy your own weapons and armor?
5. Are you able-bodied and in good health?

There is one final question to answer.
It could make a big difference:

Do you live in Sparta?

Sparta

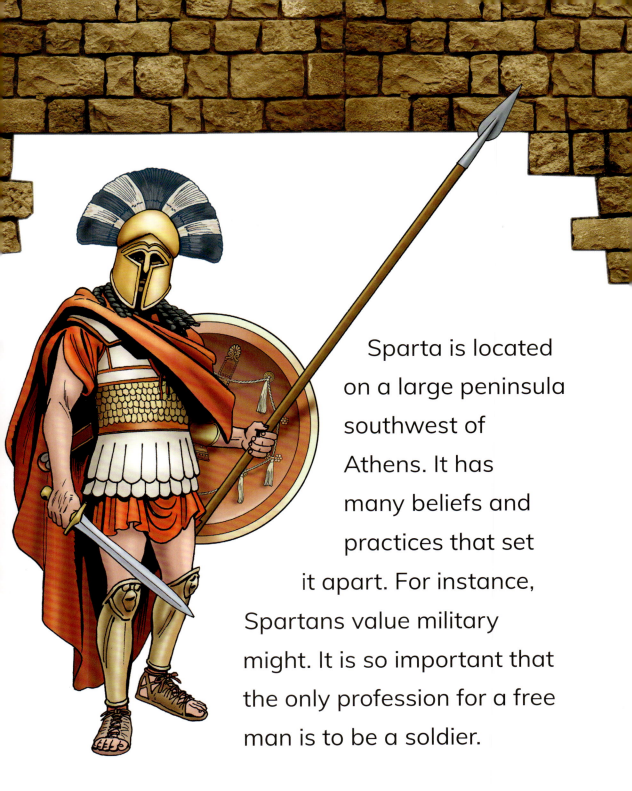

Sparta is located on a large peninsula southwest of Athens. It has many beliefs and practices that set it apart. For instance, Spartans value military might. It is so important that the only profession for a free man is to be a soldier.

Chapter 2

Training and Weapons

You grow up in Athens. Education is important. You attend school at a young age. You learn to read and write.

You are also encouraged to be fit. You do exercises and play sports to build strength and **stamina**. Running, boxing, and wrestling are a part of your daily life.

When you turn 18, your military training begins. It will last two years. At the end of your first year, you receive a sword and shield.

TIP #1: Train Like an Olympian

Many of the sports hoplites played were part of the ancient Olympic games, which began in Greece in the year 776 CE. Some of those sports—including boxing, wrestling, and running—are still part of the Olympics today.

If you live in Sparta, you will go through more **rigorous** training. It begins when you are 7 years old. The agoge is Sparta's educational and training system. It uses harsh methods.

In Sparta, boys are forced to go barefoot. They are given one cloak to wear year-round. They must make their own beds from plants torn from riverbanks.

This training continues until the age of 18. Spartans remain active soldiers until age 60.

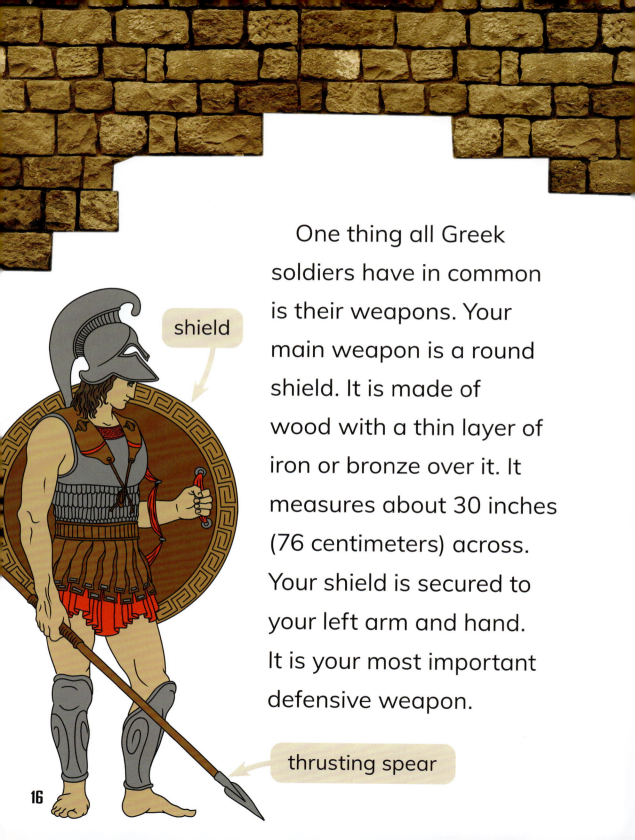

One thing all Greek soldiers have in common is their weapons. Your main weapon is a round shield. It is made of wood with a thin layer of iron or bronze over it. It measures about 30 inches (76 centimeters) across. Your shield is secured to your left arm and hand. It is your most important defensive weapon.

You carry a thrusting spear in your right hand. The spear measures about 8 feet (2.5 meters) and has a sharp iron tip. You also bring a short sword onto the battlefield. This is only used if your spear is lost or broken.

short sword

Finally, you wear armor. It consists of a helmet, chest armor, and shin guards called greaves.

Bronze armor is heavy! It weighs about 70 pounds (32 kilograms) in total.

Most hoplites are from the wealthy middle class or have jobs outside the military. Because of this, you are expected to buy your own weapons and armor. Other times, families pass armor down from one generation to the next.

TIP #2: Gear Up

A hoplite's full combination of armor and weapons was called a **panoply**. It included a shield, breastplate, helmet, sword, and spear.

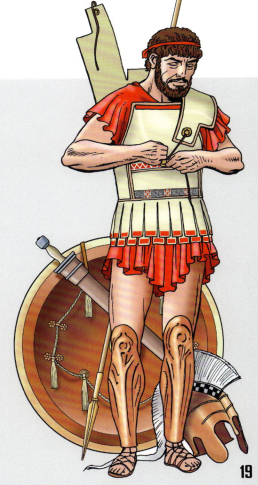

Chapter 3

Phalanx Power

The strength of the Greek army comes from a battle formation called the **phalanx**. Soldiers assemble in rows that stretch hundreds of men across. The rows are eight or more deep. These lines could stretch for more than a quarter of a mile.

Warriors stand shoulder to shoulder. This forms a wall of shields. The menacing sight gives the Greek army an advantage.

The soldiers on the far right are in the most dangerous position. They are only protected by a shield on one side. The men chosen for this position are among the most experienced fighters.

TIP #3: Left vs. Right

What if a hoplite was left-handed? It is possible left-handed soldiers were trained until they were comfortable wielding a spear with their right hand.

Hoplites are mostly foot soldiers. But there are some soldiers mounted on horses. If you earn enough to own a horse, you fight as cavalry.

These soldiers are positioned off to the sides of the phalanx. Their job is to keep enemy soldiers from taking the phalanx by surprise.

TIP #4: Join the Cavalry

The Greek word for cavalry is **hippeis**. Horses in the cavalry also wore bronze armor. But because owning a horse was expensive, this grouping of soldiers was typically small.

Chapter 4

Ready for Battle?

You are on a battlefield, ready to fight with your fellow warriors. For this battle, the armies of several city-states have joined together. You must defend the Greek empire.

The army you are up against does not use the phalanx formation. They have more soldiers mounted on horses. To your enemy, the phalanx looks like a solid wall. As you grip your spear, you hope that gives you an advantage.

On a given signal, the Greek army moves forward. Just the front rows advance at first. At the rear, you and the warriors next to you nudge those ahead onward with your spears. This ensures everyone stays together. The phalanx must stay solid. The shield wall cannot be broken.

As you march forward, you brace yourself for the clang of swords and thrusting of spears. You are ready for the fight.

But winning or losing is not up to a single soldier. You hope your fellow fighters are ready too. You will need everyone to win this battle.

Greek Warrior Test

1. Soldiers in the Greek city-state of Sparta begin training at age:
- a. 18
- b. 60
- c. 7

2. The formation used by the armies of the Greek city-states was called a:
- a. phalanx
- b. fantastic
- c. fantail

3. Two of a hoplite's main weapons are his:
- a. sword and helmet
- b. spear and shield
- c. panoply and phalanx

4. Some of the Olympic sports hoplites used in training were:
- a. skiing and snowboarding
- b. wrestling and ice skating
- c. boxing and wrestling

5. A hoplite's weapons were made of:
- a. steel
- b. pottery
- c. bronze

Answers: 1) c, 2) a, 3) b, 4) c, 5) c

If you answered all the questions correctly, you are ready to be an ancient Greek warrior! If not, take another read through this book and try the test again!

Glossary

alliance (uh-LY-uhnts)—an agreement between groups to work together

city-state (SI-tee STAYT)—a self-governing community including a town and its surrounding territory

democracy (di-MAH-kruh-see)—a form of government in which the citizens can choose their leaders

hippeis (hip-ee-UHS)—ancient Greek cavalry

hoplite (HOP-lahyt)—a Greek foot soldier

militia (muh-LISH-uh)—a group of volunteer citizens who are organized to fight, but who are not professional soldiers

panoply (PAN-uh-plee)—a hoplite's full set of weapons and armor

phalanx (FAL-angks)—a battle formation that looked like a wall of shields

rigorous (RIG-er-uhs)—difficult and disciplined

stamina (STAM-uh-nuh)—the energy and strength to keep doing something for a long time

Index

agoge, 14
alliances, 7
armor, 9, 18, 19, 25
Athens, 6, 11, 12

battles, 26, 28, 29

cavalry, 24, 25
city-states, 4, 5, 6, 7, 26

education, 12, 14

hoplites, 8, 9, 13, 19, 23, 24

jobs, 8, 19

militia, 8

Olympics, 13

panoply, 19
phalanx, 20–21, 22, 24, 26, 28

requirements, 9

Sparta, 6, 10, 11, 14, 15
sports, 12, 13

training, 13, 14, 15

weapons, 9, 16–17, 19, 21, 22, 23, 26, 28, 29

About the Author

Catherine M. Andronik is a high school teacher librarian who specializes in writing children's and young adult biographies. She shares her Connecticut home with a variety of rescue parrots and also enjoys showing her horse in western dressage.